The Cho

Secret Strategies for Overcoming

Written by Apostolic Prophetess Yvette Duffy, MSOL

Copyright Page

Scripture quotations were taken from The New Open Bible, New King James Version, Copyright 1990, 1985, 1983 by Thomas Nelson, Inc., and various Scripture resources found on the internet Google search.

Atoning Blood Ministries International

Copyright © 2024 by Yvette Duffy, Cincinnati, Ohio 45240

Printed in the United States of America. All rights reserved under the Copyright Law. Contents may not be reproduced in whole or in part without the express written consent of the author.

Dedication

This book is dedicated to all those who continually press toward the mark for the prize of the high calling; to those who continually push for righteousness in the face of adversity and keep showing up ready to battle! For those who are absolutely committed to staying on the Path of Righteousness all the days of their life until we behold Jesus, Face to face. This is the Path of HIS Chosen Ones.

Subject Background

One morning, very early while in my time of prayer and Bible study, the LORD GOD illuminated Psalm 106:4-5 which states, **"Remember me O LORD with the favor YOU have toward your people; oh, visit me with YOUR salvation, That I may see the benefit of YOUR <u>chosen ones</u>, That I may rejoice in the gladness of YOUR nation, That I may glory with YOUR inheritance."** The term **Chosen Ones** clearly stood out from the other words.

Knowing that nation means a people group (versus a Kingdom, like the United States or another country), I looked more closely at Psalm 106. It states that the Chosen Ones are God's nation and inheritance. Then **Psalm 106:23 states, "Therefore HE said that HE would destroy them, had not Moses, HIS chosen one stood before HIM in the breach."** Wait a minute, I was always taught and read in the Scripture itself that the Nation of Israel is the chosen nation, and later in the New Testament that anyone who comes to Christ Jesus is the seed of Abraham through faith, so we became a part of HIS chosen nation- through faith. But this passage of Scripture that I just read is referring to Moses separately and then destroying the Children of Israel. Could there be Chosen Ones amongst the Chosen? What a revelation! I got so excited and thus began my journey to understand who the Chosen Ones are and from verse 5, what are their benefits?

This started a whole train of thought about other Scriptures where the word chosen is used. From my studies, I have gathered that the Chosen Ones are ones selected for specific and unique purposes, assignments & missions. The Holy Spirit also gave me another understanding of the Scripture in **Matthew, verse 22:14.** It states, **"Many are called but few are chosen."** I thought about how Jesus **appointed** and sent out the group of 70 disciples, but HE said to HIS 12 chosen Apostles in **John 15:16, "You did not choose ME, but I chose you and appointed you..."** so there are two levels, appointed and chosen. But then, even out of the 12, Jesus had 3,

Peter, James and John who experienced and witnessed special times with HIM; they are often referred to as the "inner circle." So, we see from the Scriptures that some are appointed, and some are chosen and appointed, and even from HIS Chosen and appointed, Jesus still had only three that HE let in very close and spent especially personal times with HIM.

In this work, we will focus on the strategies, what the Chosen Ones did to overcome the challenging situations that arose in their lives, yet they successfully navigated and routed their enemies during these difficult times.

Reading about and learning how to apply the strategies of winning in difficult circumstances from the accounts of Chosen Ones' lives is absolutely priceless. Their methods or strategies worked and enabled each one to be an overcomer, so it would be a type of walking with the wise and growing wise as we apply each strategy to our own lives when similar situations arise to confront us.

It is my hope that as you read this book, you will be trained in the art of spiritual warfare and be equipped with new strategies to overcome the schemes of the wicked one. To be, and to always be the Overcoming Warrior that God, WHO only speaks truth, says you are.

May you too be a Chosen One,

Love, Apostolic Prophetess Yvette

CODE OF THE OVERCOMING WARRIOR

THRU THE POWER OF THE HOLY SPIRIT:

I RISE UP OUT OF MEDIOCRITY, AND I DEFEAT ALL NEGATIVITY.
LIKE A BROKEN MIRROR, I SHATTER EVERY STATISTIC,
BY PERSISTENCE, I CONQUER EVERY STEREOTYPE THAT WANTS TO CAGE ME!

WITH MY ACTIONS, I SILENCE EVERY VOICE THAT SAYS, "I CAN'T" AND I SOAR IN LIFE, UNDERGIRDED BY THE WORDS OF THE LAMB!

BY MY PRAISE TO HIM WHO IS THE ALMIGHTY, DEMONIC STRONGHOLDS GIVE WAY.
I RISE ABOVE EVERY DESTINY KILLING THOUGHT, AND ERASE EVERY NEGATIVELY SPOKEN WORD, EVER SPOKEN AGAINST ME. AND INSTEAD, I OVERCOME, AND I AM VICTORIOUS THRU THE POWER OF THE BLOOD OF THE LAMB, THAT IS CONTINUOUSLY FIGHTING FOR ME!

BY MY FASTING AND MY PRAYERS, I STAND MY GROUND AND FIGHT, FOR MY FUTURE, AND THAT OF MY FAMILY'S.

NEVER GIVING UP-I PUSH ON, SEEKING UNTIL I FIND, KNOCKING UNTIL THE DOOR OPENS!
FOR THE ONE WHO PROMISED IS FAITHFUL, AND WITH PERSISTENCE, I GAIN THE VICTORY!

WITH MY GIVING, AN ACT OF RIGHTEOUSNESS, I PLANT MANY SEEDS.
SOWING FOR MY FUTURE, AND THAT OF MY OFFSPRING, FOR HE HAS PROMISED A GREAT HARVEST THAT WILL BE REAPED BY THOSE WHO BELIEVE.

I AM AN OVERCOMING WARRIOR, I PRESS ON IN JESUS'S NAME,
FOREVER MOVING FORWARD, SENDING UP A SHOUT OF PRAISE!
WINNING VICTORY AFTER VICTORY, OVERCOMING IN HIS NAME!

Introduction

Romans 15:4: "For whatever things were written before <u>were written for our learning</u>, that we through the patience and comfort of the Scriptures might have hope."

God, knowing the battles that laid ahead for HIS Church, equipped us with HIS Word. HE inspired men to write the accounts as a record for us that we may learn from what other Chosen Ones endured and how they overcame. The Bible for us is like a time capsule; it is full of treasures from the past, golden nuggets of truths. We are to use the same secret strategies today by applying what the Holy Spirit reveals to us for our personal situations, in our time of need.

In the Lord's Prayer, Jesus said, "Thy Kingdom (dominion, authority, rule) come, Thy will be done on Earth as it is in Heaven." As God's ambassadors, we represent HIS rulership in the Earth. Through Jesus' delegated authority, we agree with, decree and declare the

Scriptures, Heaven's Words, and watch the contents of HIS Word be established in the Earth as our situations bow and give way to what The LORD GOD has spoken.

Since GOD'S Word is forever established, it is the ongoing, always existing, forever truth! Nothing can uproot it, nothing can deter it, nothing and no one has the power to change or erase it, and we have been given the right to use it!

Knowing that HE is the Almighty and that HIS Words create, we can expect to receive victory after victory as we stay steady and faithfully apply the knowledge that GOD has encapsulated for us in HIS Scriptures.

I Peter 2:9, "But you are a chosen generation, a royal priesthood, a holy nation, His own special people, that you may proclaim the praises of Him who called you out of darkness."

The Chosen Ones: Secret Strategies of Living an Overcoming LIFE!

The Warrior's Journey

Secret #1 "Be Still and <u>know</u> that I AM God" (Psalm 46:10)

Philippians 3:10 "That I might <u>know HIM</u>, and the power of HIS resurrection, and the fellowship of HIS sufferings; being made conformable to HIS death."

II Timothy 4:7 "I have fought the good fight, I have finished the race, I have kept the faith.

Secret Strategies of Apostle Paul, Chosen One

In order to know who God is in greater measures, we see from Apostle Paul's Letter to the Philippians, in chapter 3:10, that there are three levels that were revealed to him: **1) "Knowing HIM by the power of HIS resurrection,"** **2) "Knowing HIM by the fellowship of HIS sufferings,"** and **3) "Knowing HIM by being made conformable to HIS death."**

The original Greek word used in this Scripture for knowing is "ginosko." Ginosko defined here means having a personal and powerful relationship with JESUS; that includes personal interactions with HIM. This, for example, is contrasted with just knowing facts about HIM.

When you just know facts about someone and not the person himself, all you have is a list of things you know, like a grocery list. For example, some are obsessed with Hollywood personalities. A fan of a "Hollywood star" can tell you all the information about the revealed personal life of ones that they follow, yet the fan does not know the "star" personally and intimately. If the fan was introduced to the "star," the "star" would have no idea who the fan was. To know JESUS means that HE is involved in your everyday life. HE is your constant companion and confidant. HE knows you and you are getting to know HIM more and more-this is one of the main life's goal of a Chosen One. Since Chosen Ones honor and serve HIM, in all decisions, you consider if HE would approve or disapprove of your choices, and you move forward according to HIS revealed way, which is always best.

At this point, you may ask how does HE reveal HIS way? The examples that I will give you here is from my own personal experience of how HE revealed HIS ways to me. I follow HIM as HE leads me, and I always come out victorious. Yes, I had to learn from experience that GOD'S ways are always best. In the past, when I have taken my own way, most times it started out great, but later, many times I was sorry and had to repent and ask for HIS help!

I have heard HIM speak to me audibly several times. One time in particular was when HE was asking me to sacrifice something that was near and dear to my heart. I did and I wanted confirmation after a few weeks passed to know that this was what HE was really requiring of me. HE showed up in the Third Watch of the night-Midnight to three a.m.

Psalm 119:62 "At midnight I rise to praise you because of your righteous rules."

In this situation, HE was calling me to live a righteous life before HIM, so I had a choice to make. I could go my own way, or I could embrace and be obedient to what HE was asking of me. I chose HIS way, and because of the depth of my sacrifice, it caused HIM to respond in a mighty way. The Light of HIS Presence was visible in my bedroom as HE entered in. HE spoke audibly with a VOICE that sounded like a bubbling brook, and HE said to me as I was still lying on my bed, now awakened from sleep," I am pleased with your obedience, ask of ME and as HE was departing, HE said it again, "Ask of ME."

Many, many times HE has given me guidance through HIS written WORD and through HIS prophets with personal prophecies. Christian International, a true and accurate prophetic part of the Body of CHRIST, has been instrumental in my receiving of personal prophecies from the LORD, which have given me much needed sound counsel and Biblical advice and wisdom. Following the LORD'S counsel has led me to victory time and time again. As we humble ourselves and let HIM lead us, HE causes everything to work for our good! (Romans 8:28 paraphrased).

In continually building our relationship with the goal of knowing JESUS more and more, Chosen Ones stay consistent and stable in our relationship with JESUS. Our lives are not lived out based on our emotions, but instead, because of the time we spend in the written WORD of GOD, because of the time we spend in HIS Presence and talking with HIM, HE keeps causing us to be overcomers; so we keep coming to HIM because HIS WORDS work!

Our "Acts of Righteousness" that JESUS teaches in Matthew Chapter 6- our daily prayers, our fasting and giving, and of course our daily reading of the Word is our mandatory mainstays since JESUS has told us that "we do not live by bread alone, but by every Word that God speaks;" and has spoken (paraphrase of Matthew 4:4). After being born again, this is the next layer of us building our solid houses, (our lives), brick by brick upon the Rock, JESUS, who is our solid foundation; (see parable of The Two Builders in Matthew 7:24-27). We know that constantly developing this relationship with HIM is the True Way into HIS Kingdom and going farther into it, and the needed daily fellowship with HIM; an appointment that we must keep.

Additionally, Chosen Ones are not after the approval of man, but instead, we run after

HIS sweet, manifested PRESENCE and that great peace, love and joy that accompanies it. HE is the architect and builder of our successful lives as we obey. When we come into HIS PRESENCE, it's like a tributary that connects and flows with The Great River of GOD, revitalizing, refreshing and capturing strength within, causing us to stand. It also is a constant reminder that HE is always with us, and this gives us great enduring hope for no matter what we will face in the future, knowing that HE accompanies us in the battles and is always fighting for us. This is the great confidence and heartfelt satisfaction that the Chosen Ones have in knowing that we are pleasing HIM.

We have this great access to JESUS the CHRIST, because after HIS Resurrection, HE became a life-giving Spirit.

I Corinthians 15: 45 states, "And so it is written, 'The first man Adam became a living being,' the last Adam, became a life-giving spirit." And in I Corinthians 15:22,

"For as in Adam all die, even so in Christ all shall be made alive."

Acts 17:28, "... in Him we live and move and have our being, as also some of your own poets have said, 'For we are also His offspring.'

****

Saul becomes Paul through the Life-Giving Spirit

Saul, although highly educated, was completely lost and on the wrong road in life; he even believed that by persecuting the Church, he was working for The LORD GoD. He was fighting a good fight, but it was the wrong fight; he was helping the enemy to destroy the Church; but the LORD had a good plan and specific assignments for Saul's life.

Jeremiah 29:11, "For I know the thoughts that I think toward you, says the Lord,

thoughts of peace and not of evil, to give you a future and a hope."

Jeremiah 1:5, "Before I formed you in the womb I knew you; Before you were born I sanctified you; And I ordained you a prophet to the nations."

Saul was arrested by the revealed manifested presence of JESUS CHRIST. Sauls life, like many of our lives, was headed in the wrong direction until JESUS, the Life-giving Spirit, interrupted our man-made plans and revealed HIMSELF to each one of us.

Saul the Pharisee, was so zealous for the religion of his ancestors. It was the way he was brought up and it was the only way he considered to be the correct way for the Jewish nation to worship GOD. Saul had to be blinded by "The Truth" in order for him to know GOD and not religion; to see the right path and receive his ministry work, as recorded in Acts chapter 9:5,8-9.

In verse 5, after the light shone around him from heaven and Saul fell to the ground, Saul cried out, **"...who are you Lord?"** This was the beginning of Saul's revelation of JESUS. It is also interesting to note that light in the Hebrew language also means revelation knowledge.

This was Saul's first encounter with HIS all-surpassing power, which is Level Number 1- **"Knowing HIM in the power of HIS resurrection."**

To backtrack for a moment, in **John 11:25-26**, JESUS had previously revealed that HE is the resurrection and the life. It states, **"Jesus said to her (Lazarus' sister), "I am the resurrection and the life. He who believes in ME, though he may die, he shall live. And whoever lives and believes in ME, shall never die..."**

The day that Saul had his first encounter with JESUS, Saul the murderer died, and Apostle Paul was resurrected; his spirit man was born again-he experienced CHRIST'S true resurrection power in his own life. Paul explained this radical life changing moment in **Galatians 2:20,** he stated **"I have been crucified with Christ; it is no longer I who live, but Christ lives in me; and the life which I now live in the flesh I live by faith in the Son of God, who loved me and gave Himself for me."**

Chosen Ones have experienced the resurrection power of CHRIST and are now born again. The lives the Chosen Ones are now living, are by faith in HIM. We have become partakers and witnesses of HIS mighty transformative power, that just like Saul, who experienced such a radical change in that moment where the heavens opened over his life, as Chosen Ones, we too have experienced radical changes that have set the whole course of our lives in a different direction.

John 12: 25-26, states **"He who loves his life will lose it, and he who hates his life in this world will keep it for eternal life. If anyone serves ME, let him follow Me; and where I am, there my servant will be also. If anyone serves Me, him My Father will honor."**

We are no longer zealous for the things of this world, but instead zeal for HIS House consumes us.

Throughout Paul's personal ministry, he experienced many hardships, which brings us to Level Number Two. At Level Number Two- **"Knowing HIM and the fellowship of HIS sufferings,"** Paul wrote of the many sufferings that he encountered; in **II Corinthians 11:24-27,** he states **"From the Jews five times I received forty stripes minus one. Three times I was beaten with rods; once I was stoned; three times I was shipwrecked; a night and a day I have been in the deep; in journeys often, in perils of waters, in perils of robbers, in perils of my own countrymen, in perils of the Gentiles, in perils in the city, in perils in the wilderness, in perils in the sea, in perils among false brethren, in weariness and toil, in sleeplessness often, in hunger and thirst, in fastings often, in cold and nakedness."** In **Colossians 1:24** Paul stated**," I now rejoice in my sufferings for you, and fill up my flesh, what is lacking in the afflictions of Christ, for the sake of HIS body, which is the church."

As a Chosen One, you too will be called upon to suffer; suffering is a promotion to the second level of "Knowing Him". JESUS said in **John 16:33, "These things I have spoken to you, that in ME you may have peace. In the world <u>you will have</u> tribulation; but be of good cheer, I have overcome the world."**

The severity of your suffering of course is up to the FATHER and the assignment that HE has chosen for your life. Chosen Ones, just as suffering was assigned to JESUS, are willing to "Drink from HIS Cup," since this is what the FATHER has willed for each of us. Chosen Ones are willing to suffer for the sake of HIS name and for HIS Kingdom purposes, for we have found a greater purpose for living, we have realized that there is no other life for us except that life that HE has chosen.

Philippians 2:29 states, "For to you it has been granted on behalf of Christ, not only to

believe in Him, but also to suffer for His sake."

And 1 Peter 4:1-2 states, "Therefore since Christ suffered for us in the flesh, arm yourselves also with the same mind, for he who has suffered in the flesh has ceased from sin, that he no longer should live the rest of his time in the flesh for the lusts of men, but for the will of God."

When a season of suffering rolls in, Chosen Ones, like Apostle Paul, fast and pray their way through it; this is the correct response of the Chosen Ones to tribulation instead of getting offended at our FATHER and murmuring and complaining. Your correct response will lead you to a closer relationship with JESUS and also an expansion of your mission and vision which God reveals in HIS time.

Acts 9:8-9, "Then Saul arose from the ground, and when his eyes were opened he saw no one. But they led him by the hand and brought him into Damascus. And he was three days without sight, and neither ate nor drank."

Saul, during his initial meeting with The LORD, was also given his next set of directions, his next steps, to paraphrase the account, Paul was told by JESUS to go on ahead into the city of Damascus where he was initially headed, and there JESUS would give him even further instructions; Saul was being led by the Holy Spirit.

Galatians 5:24-25 states, "And those who are Christ's have crucified the flesh with its passions and desires, If we live in the Spirit, let us also walk in the Spirit.

And Romans 8:14, "For as many as are led by the Spirit of God, these are the sons of God."

Chosen Ones are obedient to the Word of God and the promptings of the Holy Spirit. I have learned by experience, that JESUS is always right in everything HE says and does. We must daily crucify our flesh by not giving in to the cravings of the lusts of the eye, lusts of the flesh and the pride of life and doing things our way; but instead, we expand GOD'S Kingdom here on earth by doing as our LORD asks. In our day-to-day living, the Holy Spirit will speak in different ways to aid you in keeping your relationship with JESUS close and intact. The Chosen Ones listen, trust and obey.

Level Number Three, **"Knowing HIM by being made conformable unto HIS death,"** speaks of our being conformed into HIS Image and likeness. Chosen Ones are consistently being transformed more and more into the image of JESUS CHRIST. CHRIST'S ways of living, HIS ability to subject HIMSELF to the will of the FATHER, even unto death, are revealed at greater levels, as the Scripture unfolds itself to us and we gain a greater understanding of Who HE is and how we should pattern our lives to be more like HIM, in order to please our FATHER. JESUS held back nothing; whatever the FATHER asked, JESUS' response was "Yes."

Hebrews 10:9 states:
"then He said, "Behold, I have come to do Your will, O God." He takes away the first (covenant) that He may establish the second (covenant). By that will we have been sanctified through the offering of the body of Jesus Christ once *for all*."

Likewise, our obedience to do whatever GOD asks of us, just like JESUS, is of paramount importance to the increasing of GOD'S Kingdom here on earth; through our obedience HE is glorified and lifted up in our lives; as HE is lifted up in our lives, HE will draw others to HIM, (see **John 12:32** below).

Philippians 2:8 states, "And being found in appearance as a man, HE humbled HIMSELF and <u>became obedient</u> to the point of death, even the death of the cross."

John 12:32 states, "And I, if I am lifted up from the earth, will draw all *peoples* to Myself."

It was this lifting of HIS Body as a peace offering that allows us to be drawn back into GOD'S Presence. Since this is the goal of JESUS, **"to draw all men,"** it automatically becomes the goal of the Chosen Ones, to draw all men to JESUS.

Since our major goals are to know HIM more and more and to be like HIM, Chosen Ones strive to be in the center of GOD'S agenda for their lives at all times.

At times, the things that The LORD asks us to do will be challenging and our circumstances will certainly at times try us, but we choose to pick up the mantra of JESUS in **Luke 22:42, "saying, 'Father, if it is Your will, take this cup away from Me; <u>nevertheless</u> not My will, but Yours, be done.'"**

In Romans 12:12, Apostle Paul encourages us to live above our present circumstances by **"rejoicing in hope,** (being) **patient in tribulation, continuing steadfast in prayer."**

Saul during his encounter with JESUS, was blinded for a period of time. We can glean this strategy from Saul's situation: *the world and all its distractions were shut out; it was just Saul and JESUS. This enabled Saul to hear from Heaven regarding his assignment clearly. When we spend time alone with HIM, we are being still before HIM. All of the distractions from all the responsibilities and other things that pull on us for our attention, just like Saul, are shut out; our focus is wholly on JESUS. It is in this time of stillness before HIM, seeking HIM only, completely focused on HIM alone, that HE will speak.

Matthew 13:16, "But blessed are your eyes for they see, and your ears for they hear;"

Luke 9:32, "But Peter and those with Him were heavy with sleep; and when they were fully awake, they saw HIS glory and the two men who stood with HIM."

Open eyes are symbolic of understanding. Our spiritual eyes are reopened when we are born again, (the day that Adam and Eve ate the fruit, their spirit man died, so their spiritual eyes were closed, and their carnal eyes were opened. Therefore, now all mankind born through them, would now be created in this carnal image, see **Genesis 5:3**), we will be able to see more and more of GOD'S glory in our personal lives as we are transformed more and more into HIS image and likeness.

We set ourselves up to receive more revelation knowledge from HIM which in turn allows us to know HIM more. Our eyes are becoming fully awake. HE may give you a new revelation from HIS Word as you read; HE may speak inwardly, in your spirit in the small still voice with correction; HE can also use your present circumstances to convey a life-changing message to you. There is a myriad of ways that HE can speak to you with the goal of creating a more personal and intimate relationship with you, giving you greater understanding of who HE truly is.

Since Saul's spiritual eyes were opened from his encounter with JESUS, <u>after</u> fasting and praying, Saul had a vision where he saw a man coming to pray for him. *Spending time in fasting and prayer will increase our spiritual capacity to see and hear in the spiritual realm. Here in the Scripture, we see that The LORD distinctly showed Paul the man who was coming to pray for him; this is a use of the Gift of The Word of Knowledge which was now operating in Paul's life.

During the same time period, while Saul (he was still called Saul in this Scripture), was in this time of consecration, the man whom he saw in the vision, Ananias, was also given a vision where the LORD gave him instructions to go and pray for Saul. The LORD also revealed to Ananias, Saul's true identity.

Ananias is what we call a destiny helper; he was sent to Saul to help him, to pray for him and to give Saul the Word of the LORD.

Acts 9:15," But the Lord said to him, (Ananias),'Go, for he (Saul) is a <u>chosen vessel</u> of Mine to bear MY NAME before Gentiles, kings and the children of Israel."

In order for our true identity and our official assignment as a Chosen One to be revealed to us; in order for us to see as GOD wants us to see with understanding, and in order for us to walk <u>with</u> GOD and be in HIS timing and for our lives to line up with HIS timetable, it will require times of "being still," before HIM; it will require that we enter into times of fasting and praying before HIM. We do not want to be "zealously working for GOD," doing whatever sounds good to us as Saul did in his previous life, but instead, we want to ensure that we are completing the specific work that HE has set us apart for. We choose to be effective, not just busy. Through prayer, GOD will also send our destiny helpers-those HE has chosen to help us in our assignments, thereby fulfilling their own.

Apostle Paul's life as a Chosen One, was completely focused on his assignment. He followed the leading of the HOLY SPIRIT even in his dealings with other members of CHRIST Church. In **Galatians 1:16-23,** after Paul was born again, he did not go straight away and meet with the other Apostles, looking for acceptance from them, but instead, like JESUS after HE was baptized, Paul followed the leading of the HOLY SPIRIT.

"**But when it pleased God, who separated me from my mother's womb and called me through His grace, to reveal His Son in me, that I might preach Him among the Gentiles, I did not immediately confer with flesh and blood, nor did I go up to Jerusalem to those** who were **apostles before me; but I went to Arabia, and returned again to Damascus."**

"Then after three years I went up to Jerusalem to see Peter and remained with him fifteen days. But I saw none of the other apostles except James, the Lord's brother. (Now *concerning* the things which I write to you, indeed, before God, I do not lie.)"

"Afterward I went into the regions of Syria and Cilicia. And I was unknown by face to the churches of Judea which *were* in Christ. But they were hearing only, "He who formerly persecuted us now preaches the faith which he once *tried to destroy.*"

Apostle Paul was busy at work with the assignment that he had received from JESUS. Chosen Ones are not busy trying to be popular in the Church, accepting every invitation to minister, running ourselves ragged to attend every social event offered by our brothers and sisters in CHRIST, in order to be a part of the "in crowd". It is not possible, nor is it beneficial to attend every offered event; we must use our time wisely. Chosen Ones are on a mission and have an assignment to complete. When the HOLY SPIRIT says "yes," then you may attend but when HE says "no," you obey and do not go. When you read the above Scriptures regarding Paul, it shows that he was focused on preaching the faith to the Gentiles. His top priority in life was to complete the work that JESUS had given him to do. Paul was not concerned with being a church socialite.

*As a Chosen One, we must also set the work of the LORD in its correct position in our lives; we give it top priority.

Since we also know that we will have to give an account for our work as clearly shown in the parable of the Good Steward in **Luke 12:35-48,** Chosen Ones work with a spirit of excellence, being faithful to all that the LORD GOD asks of us.

I Corinthians 3:13-15 states, **"each one's work will become clear; for the Day will declare it, because it will be revealed by fire; and the fire will test each one's work, of what sort it is. If anyone's work which he has built on it endures, he will receive a reward. If anyone's work is burned, he will suffer loss; but he himself will be saved, yet so as through fire."**

JESUS said in **John 17:4,** "I have glorified YOU on the earth. I have finished the work which YOU have given ME to do." We too will bring HIM glory in the earth by completing the work that HE has given us to do. **Colossians 3:23-24** states, "Whatever you do, work heartily, as for the Lord and not for men, knowing that from the Lord, you'll receive the inheritance as your reward. You are serving the Lord Christ."

Eventually, just like Apostle Paul, we will be able to say as he said in **II Timothy 4:7-8**, "I have fought the good fight, I have finished the race, I have kept the faith. Finally there is laid up for me the crown of righteousness, which the LORD, the righteous Judge, will give to me on that Day, and not to me only but also to all who have loved HIS appearing."

Secret #2 Never Count yourself Out!

Apostle Peter, Chosen One

II Corinthians 12:9, "And HE said to me, 'My grace is sufficient for you. For MY strength is made perfect in weakness.'"

We want to be perfect, but at times we will fall short. When these occasions of falling short of what God wanted us to be or to accomplish occurs, it is vital that we do not count ourselves out. Instead, we must repent, stand up and keep moving forward. For a Chosen One, this is the way.

GOD'S grace is sufficient for us. I am so very glad that GOD included this Scripture in the Bible; it is a fail-safe for us. It reminds me of a rollercoaster ride at an amusement park; usually there is a seatbelt, as well as a safety bar in each seat. If one fails, there is a backup to keep us in place. From Apostle Peter's life, we see that he failed JESUS by not acknowledging HIM in front of men, but instead, denying HIM in front of men. After Peter realized that he had failed his LORD, and had denied HIM, just as JESUS had prophesied -three times before the rooster crowed- the Scripture records that "**Peter wept bitterly,"** see **Matthew 26:75.**

I can just imagine how disappointed Peter was with himself; how he knew that when JESUS needed him the most, he had failed HIM. When you read the whole account, Peter was so sure that he would never betray JESUS. We can feel the same way, standing strong, so self-assured and then BAM! We fall into the test. It often overtakes us without prior notice, and then, so often, we fail. The enigma concerning Peter's test, is that JESUS HIMSELF told Peter what actions that Peter would take. In light of this, you would probably guess that since Peter had the information ahead of time, that he would do differently and not deny JESUS, and pass the test; yet, this was not the case.

I Corinthians 3:12, "Therefore let him who thinks he stands take heed lest he fall."

When we fail, we can be so very hard on ourselves, feeling like we will never measure up, so we may just as well forget trying. JESUS shows us, in this real-life circumstance, how forgiving and loving that HE really is. We know from the Scriptures, that JESUS experienced emotions like any other human, so when one of HIS closest companions denied HIM not once, but three times, the pain of hurt and rejection most likely cut deep into JESUS' heart. Many of us, if we were in a situation where we had just been denied and rejected, would have cut the person/people out of our lives who offended us, but that was not JESUS' way nor HIS reaction.

Breakfast by the Sea

John 21:1-17 "After these things Jesus showed Himself again to the disciples at the Sea of Tiberias, and in this way He showed *Himself:* Simon Peter, Thomas called the Twin, Nathanael of Cana in

Galilee, the *sons* of Zebedee, and two others of His disciples were together.

Simon Peter said to them, "I am going fishing."

"They said to him, "We are going with you also." They went out and immediately got into the boat, and that night they caught nothing. But when the morning had now come, Jesus stood on the shore; yet the disciples did not know that it was Jesus. Then Jesus said to them, "Children, have you any food?"

They answered Him, "No."

And He said to them, "Cast the net on the right side of the boat, and you will find *some*." So they cast, and now they were not able to draw it in because of the multitude of fish."

"Therefore that disciple whom Jesus loved said to Peter, 'It is the Lord!' Now when Simon Peter heard that it was the Lord, he put on *his* outer garment (for he had removed it) and plunged into the sea. ⁸ But the other disciples came in the little boat (for they were not far from land, but about two hundred cubits), dragging the net with fish. Then, as soon as they had come to land, they saw a fire of coals there, and fish laid on it, and bread. Jesus said to them, "Bring some of the fish which you have just caught."

"Simon Peter went up and dragged the net to land, full of large fish, one hundred and fifty-three; and although there were so many, the net was not broken. Jesus said to them, 'Come and eat breakfast.' Yet none of the disciples dared ask Him, 'Who are You?'—knowing that it was the Lord. Jesus then came and took the bread and gave it to them, and likewise the fish."

"This is now the third time Jesus showed Himself to His disciples after He was raised from the dead."

Jesus Restores Peter

"So when they had eaten breakfast, Jesus said to Simon Peter, 'Simon, son of Jonah, do you love Me more than these?'"

"He said to Him, 'Yes, Lord; You know that I love You.'"

"He said to him, 'Feed My lambs.'"

"He said to him again a second time, 'Simon, *son* of Jonah, do you love Me?'"

"He said to Him, 'Yes, Lord; You know that I love You.'"

"He said to him, 'Tend My sheep.'"

"He said to him the third time, 'Simon, *son* of Jonah, do you love Me?' Peter was grieved because He said to him the third time, 'Do you love Me?'"

"And he said to Him, 'Lord, You know all things; You know that I love You.'"

"Jesus said to him, 'Feed My sheep.'"

Before JESUS restored Peter, Peter most likely thought to himself, HE will never forgive me for this, what use am I now? I am sure all the disciples have heard what I did. Surely Peter was very ashamed and maybe even embarrassed to face JESUS again.

But, before we are too hard on Apostle Peter, we must ask ourselves, how many times have we ever denied CHRIST by our actions, by our own words. As Chosen Ones, we must choose to live holy no matter what. I heard a person once say, "on Saturday night it's our night, I can do what I want to do, but on Sunday, I will go to church." JESUS is our GOD every single day. What we do on any given day, at any given time, will reflect on HIS Church. HIS Blood purchased us, and we belong to HIM, no matter what day of the week it is.

We must always rely on JESUS for the strength and grace that HE provides to admit that we were wrong. We must quickly repent, ask the LORD GOD for help to make it through the test, and to restore our relationship with HIM when we fail. We cannot turn away from our GOD, letting pride enter into our hearts-pride is a trap! The enemy know the Scriptures too and has designed pride to destroy you. Destruction follows on the heels of pride, (**Proverbs 16:18**); we must humble ourselves before HIM, see **James 4:10**.

JESUS in HIS great mercy, compassion, and love that HE has for each one of us, when we have fallen short, also showed those same attributes to Peter, and did not count him out. Instead, HE restored Peter to HIS leadership position. HE is absolutely the GOD of another chance.

II Corinthians 12:9, "And HE said to me, 'My grace is sufficient for you. For MY strength is made perfect in weakness.'"

Ephesians 4:1-3 states, "I, therefore, the prisoner of the Lord, beseech you to walk worthy of the calling with which you were called, with all lowliness and gentleness, with longsuffering, bearing with one another in love, endeavoring to keep the unity of the Spirit in the bond of peace."

I believe Peter was utterly devasted. Just a little while before Peter spoke and denied JESUS, Peter had promised JESUS that if all fell away, he never would. I also believe that at the time Peter spoke those words, that he really meant them. He was so zealous for JESUS- he was the one walking on the water, he was the one willing to fight for JESUS as shown by his cutting off the ear of the high priests' servant in the Garden of Gethsemane when the mob, led by Judas, came to take JESUS away. Peter loved JESUS-now, he had failed HIM by denying that he even knew HIM, not once, not twice, but three times- all in the same night.

One of my most favorite pastors, once while preaching said, "the worst things that you could ever do is to count yourself out. If GOD hasn't counted you out, then you're still in!" I have learned that this is so true. Never give up on yourself, GOD hasn't given up on you and HE is all-powerful, the Almighty! If HE said you can do it, then you can. HE will be there to forgive you and restore you too, just like HE did for Peter.

Some years ago, like Peter, I quit and walked away from the ministry. I felt that I had suffered much, been so mistreated by my sisters and brothers in Christ. I had been lied on and rejected many times and I was tired of it. I even told the LORD, "If these are Your people, YOU can keep them." I still wanted to belong to HIM though, as a part of HIS Church, because from all the experiences that I had with CHRIST, I couldn't erase them as if they never existed. I loved HIM so much, but I didn't want to minister anymore, anywhere.

On Sunday mornings, I begin listening to a well-known pastor. GOD was definitely speaking to me every single Sunday through this man of GOD. During this same period of time, I had recently made a new friend; she is one of the sweetest people that I have ever met even to this day. She invited me and my husband to visit her church. We did, and boy, did GOD make use of those visits! The pastor's words cut at my heart. One Sunday morning, a personal prayer that I had just prayed to our FATHER before leaving out for church, the same words, literally, the same exact words came out of his mouth at altar call time. There was now, no doubt, that JESUS was calling me back; HE had a purpose for my life, a destiny waiting to be fulfilled, so I couldn't, I didn't, want to resist HIM any longer.

HE saved me again at one of the lowest point in my life. HE also has done so many miracles for me and my family-so when HE started reaching out to me, like Peter, I wanted JESUS back, to walk closely with HIM again as in times past. HE began to restore me and eventually HE asked me to start Atoning Blood Ministries, International, to which I said "yes!" never wanting to let HIM down again.

Through this situation, just as JESUS told Peter, "Follow ME," I realized that it was not a man that I was following, but JESUS CHRIST Himself. Now, even though there has been many challenges since, and times where I have had to forgive and show love and mercy to those who have wounded me; when the offense, the pain hits my heart, I have learned to quickly forgive. I never want to be separated from HIM again, so I do what HE commands me. My life is nothing, an empty shell without HIM and I do not want to spend even five minutes with sin separating me from HIM. I forgive and HE forgives me when I fall short, just as the Scripture says.

If you have made mistakes and wrong choices, even if you have walked away from HIM in shame, not serving GOD anymore like you once did, like Peter, HE will give you a second chance. Don't count yourself out! In HIS mercy, HE will absolutely forgive you and restore you as shown in Apostle Peter's life. HE is just that loving and kind.

*Chosen Ones have learned to repent instead of letting pride build a wall between them and God. Chosen Ones walk humbly before HIM, knowing that any other life, is an empty life. We cannot let anything separate us from HIM.

Maybe you are getting tired of the way that people are treating you; maybe you have experienced so much church hurt that you have lost faith in your brothers and sisters in CHRIST. That is the problem!

Your faith should be in GOD! *We must stay focused on JESUS and our own personal walk with HIM. JESUS' reply to Peter in **John 21:22** applies to you too "...**you follow Me.**"

As a Chosen One, when the challenging times show up, because you have founded your life on the ROCK, CHRIST JESUS, not the pastor, not the other saints of GOD, the storms that roll into your life will not be able to shake you loose from your relationship with HIM. When Peter asked JESUS to let him walk on the water, Peter was doing just fine until he started to look around. He lost his focus, and it caused him to sink. Sometimes life's challenges will make you feel as if you are sinking; they can make you feel like you want to give up, to quit. This is exactly the way that the adversary wants you to feel so that you will walk away from JESUS! Keep your focus on JESUS.

Never count yourself out, never quit! Learn the secret of taking life one day at a time, one decision at a time!

Taking life one day at a time, is to be focused on "just today." Today I will live right, today I will serve the LORD, today I will choose right over wrong. Then when the evening comes, you will have had another successful, victorious day in CHRIST JESUS.

Please know that these situations may also be a testing of your faith; we all go through tests. The Word says in **John 1:11, "HE came to HIS own, and HIS own did not receive HIM."** Even JESUS HIMSELF faced rejection and persecution. The LORD is testing you to see if you will be faithful to HIM no matter what the circumstances; this is a part of Level 2, and Level 3 **"sharing in the fellowship of HIS sufferings,"** and **"being conformable to HIS death"** as shown by our obedience. Will you stand in and for HIM, trust HIM and believe HIS Word or will you walk away?

After returning and picking up the call again, yes, I have had to endure many challenges, underhanded insults, insults to my face, betrayal and many other things that we would label as a hardship or a challenge. But, in **Hebrews 12:4 it states, "You have not yet resisted to bloodshed in your striving against sin."** Most of us have not given one drop of blood for the cause of CHRIST. Chosen Ones must remember **Romans 8:28, it states," And we know that all things work together for good to those who love God, to those who are called according to his purpose.."** Everything, every challenge, every test, every battle, each victory, each failure we have in life, HE uses it to conform us into HIS image.

Just as in Peter's restoration, the LORD will restore you too. In fact, we also find this same pattern in the Old Testament.

There is a day of second chances with God as illustrated through the establishing of the Second Passover. In the Book of Numbers 9:6-7, we read that some of the Israelite's were ceremonially unclean and were unable to keep the original and first Passover on Nissan 14 (Numbers 9:2-3). The second Passover is called Pesach Sheni; it is the Day of Second Chances. This shows us that God will forgive us and "Passover" the mistakes that we have made and give us another opportunity to make it right. GOD is so good; we love HIM for HIS mercy and kindness toward us. **Never count yourself out**! If GOD says, "you're in," then you're in. HIS grace is sufficient for us!

Secret #3 Turn Aside!

Chosen One: King David

"I wished I had, I knew I should of, if only I would have… These are the statements of those who missed the target and ended up with less than what GOD had purposed for their lives.

In **1 Samuel 17**, we find the account of David. His dad sent him to check on his brothers who were in the army and battling the Philistines. David heard what the men, in fear, were saying about the Philistine champion, the giant Goliath; but David also heard what the then King of Israel, Saul, promised to the man that would defeat the giant.

David's eldest brother, Eliab, heard David asking about the King's gifts to the victor of the slain giant, and he got upset with David. **He said, in verse 28 "Why did you come down here? And with whom have you left those few sheep in the wilderness? I know your pride and the naughtiness of your** heart; for you came so that you could see the battle." David replied, 'what have I now done? Is there not a cause?'" **Verse 30** gives us the invaluable, gold nugget of information of what David did; it states in **Verse 30, "And he turned from him toward another.."**

*There will be times in your life, in order to attain to the height of the destiny that GOD has for you, that you will have to turn aside, just like David, from the ones who are critical of you.

From David's account, my own experience and in talking with others down through the years, it seems when you want to move ahead in life, the doubters show up informing you of what you cannot do. Usually, the general direction of the conversation consists of spewing out all the challenges that will come against you and what you want to achieve. Sometimes there is even slander against you involved; this is designed to demoralize you and keep you from moving forward. The conversation usually ends with, "if I were you I wouldn't..." That person is not you, so therefore you cannot apply their negative advice to your life. Turn Aside!

Isaiah 53:1, "Who has believed our report? And to whom has the arm of the LORD been revealed?"

The Hebrew word translated report is **shemuswah**, which means the report that reached us. **Zerowa**, in Hebrew means Divine Strength.

Although David was a young man, he already had experienced the Divine Strength of the ALMIGHTY in his life. In his experiences with HIM, David was enabled to kill a lion and to kill a bear as he guarded the flock entrusted to his care. David absolutely believed that the ALMIGHTY would show up again to deliver HIS flock, Israel from the enemy.

*Along the way, you will learn that you absolutely have to let some people go. The naysayers will surely try to get you to give up. In David's case, it was his own family member who was speaking against him.

Matthew 10:36 states, "and a man's enemies will be those of his own household."

Those in your own household often know you best, your strengths, your weaknesses, your dreams.

I received a personal prophetic word that said the LORD was going to allow me to go to a place that I wanted so badly to go-it was Israel. The prophetic word went on to say that the LORD was going to open the door and allow me to go. In 2009, the opportunity presented itself. The LORD miraculously blessed me with the funding to pay for the trip and money to spend while abroad. I was so excited, another prophetic word coming to pass! One of my family members who held a position of influence within the family tried to throw a guilt trip on me to keep me from going. I heard exactly what they said, I looked at them and said, "I sure am going." Just like David, I had to turn aside and not let their words, their opinion sway me into doing differently. God had provided the opportunity, and I was not about to let it pass me by. I had the absolute most wonderful time; I was even baptized in the Jordan River. After returning home, I had the picture of my baptism blown up very large; it is still on the wall in my home to this very day; a continual reminder of the goodness, the faithfulness of our FATHER.

Recently, I have often thought about Apostle Andrew, Peter's brother; he was not a part of the "inner circle," but his brother Peter was. Peter had to choose to move ahead without his brother. Peter couldn't allow family ties to dictate his path in life. Peter and two other disciples were allowed to experience especially special times with JESUS. Do not allow others to kill your GOD-given destiny. Turn Aside! David was already a warrior, he had already experienced what he could do with GOD'S help; it was absolutely too late for his brother to tell him to go back home, David knew who he was.

When The LORD created you, as your manufacturer, HE put in you all the specifications, all the qualifications, gifts and talents that you will need in order to fulfill your purpose, the reason HE sent you to planet Earth. As a Chosen One, you are well able to complete your mission. *The key is to stay focused, stay on track no matter what! The enemy will definitely send some to plant seeds of doubt, some to plant seeds of rejection, some to make you feel as if you cannot overcome- sometimes they sound so reasonable by saying, "just cut your losses now before you lose more." The one I see most often is distraction-whether it is good or bad.

*One strategy that I employ is that I have overcome many distractions by having a plan and sticking to it, no matter what.

Your moving forward in the LORD will definitely rub some the wrong way, but in order to succeed in your mission for HIM, some will absolutely have to fall by the wayside in your life.

"Be strong in the LORD and in the power of HIS might," (see Ephesians 6:10).

Do not give in to the naysayers, turn aside! Your path in life isn't anyone else's path. This is the main reason why they cannot see how it could work. I always say everyone has a mouth, and they are going to use it. They are going to talk whether it is good or bad, for you or against you, everyone has their own opinion. *BUT! The only opinion that truly counts is what does GOD say about you? Whose report will you believe? Who does HE say that you are? What dreams do you have that HE has placed inside you? What plans have you considered and would love to fulfill for your life's journey here? I love **Jeremiah 29:11,** it was quoted earlier but bears quoting again, it states, **"For I know the plans I have for you, declares the LORD, plans to prosper you and not to harm you, plans to give you a hope and a future."** The LORD has a great future planned for you.

*As you remain faithful to HIM, just like our example written in Scripture regarding

Abraham's life; as we are faithful, The LORD will reveal HIS plan to us in part. As we continue to be faithful to HIM and complete the part that HE has revealed to us, HIS plan continues to roll out in our lives. As we are faithful to carry out HIS directives, it will cause us to succeed and have a fulfilled life. Turn Aside!

Secret #4 Do what HE tells you!
(John 2:5)

Chosen One: Mary, Jesus' Mom & King Saul

One of the easiest ways to hear GOD and to get to know HIM better is through a regular daily reading of The Bible. The Bible is full of instructions and excellent advice. As you get to know GOD better, you will develop a sensing in your spirit man of HIS ways. The excellent news is that HE never changes, so once HE reveals a truth to you, it's a truth that you can stand on forever!

In John 2:5, Mary, JESUS' mom, gave excellent advice that rang true down the ages of time and still rings true even today. She and her Son, JESUS, amongst others, were at a wedding. The hosts ran out of wine. Mary, to save the host from an embarrassing situation, asked JESUS to help. From the Text, there doesn't seem to be any stores around or guests bearing extra wine jars. From JESUS' reply to His mom, it seems HE was very reluctant to help. It would have been very easy for Mary to give up. Instead, even though she heard what her SON said, Mary looked at the servants and told them to do whatever JESUS told them to do. Mary knew her SON, she had received information of who HE was going to be from an angelic visitation before HIS miraculous birth. She knew that HE was conceived by a miracle, that HE was and is a miracle and that HE is the miracle-worker. Even though JESUS had told HIS mom that it wasn't time yet for HIS miracle ministry, the faith of Mary and the relationship between them, caused JESUS to move, even though HE said HIMSELF, it was out of timing. See what obedience will do for you?

*When The LORD looks at your record of faith and obedience, it will cause miracles to show up in your life.

In contrast, we must also look at the cost of being disobedient. So many people pick and choose what commands of GOD that they will obey, and what commands of GOD that they are not going to obey. The cost of disobedience can be very high and cause your blessing that was earmarked for you, to be transferred to another.

In the **Book of I Samuel chapter 9-10,** is the account of a man born in the tribe of Benjamin, so a Benjamite. The Bible records that he was an impressive young man without equal amongst all the Israelites. The LORD GOD chose this man... what an honor! Hand-picked by GOD HIMSELF from amongst all the people of the whole nation of Israel to be anointed as its first mortal king; **I Samuel 9:1, 9:15-17, 10:1.**

The LORD sent HIS Prophet Samuel, to anoint Saul. What great joy must have flooded Saul's heart-he was anointed and chosen by GOD HIMSELF. He-Saul would be king and that meant his offspring, each of his sons, would be a prince-one of which would be next in line to inherit the throne; his family had just become royalty!

What a glorious day it must have been for Saul and his father's house. How proud Saul's father must have been of his son, his own son, chosen by The Great JEHOVAH to lead the nation, the only people on earth called by HIS Holy Name.

After Saul was anointed, the Prophet Samuel, gave King Saul the instructions from Heaven. GOD was testing Saul, testing Saul's patience and Saul's obedience to HIS Word.

In the Book of 1 Samuel chapter 10:8, Samuel said to Saul, "wait for me seven days and I will come and I will offer up the fellowship and burnt offerings to God," clear instructions. Around the 7th day, Saul got so impatient, he decided to offer up the offerings himself. Now according to the Old Covenant, the Law given by JEHOVAH God to HIS people Israel, **(Leviticus chapters 6 &7)** to paraphrase, it says that only the priests were allowed to offer the offerings to GOD because they had been set apart by HIM for this sacred duty. How could Saul ever think that he was above GOD'S Law? As King, he should have been the first partaker, the first to do what GOD had commanded, to show the nation how to honor GOD through patient obedience.

 But Saul, Saul became impatient as he waited for Samuel; and wouldn't you know it? Just as Saul finished offering the sacrifices, Samuel arrived. Samuel looked and saw the remains of the offering and asked Saul, **"what have you done?" 1 Samuel 13:13, "And Samuel said to Saul, 'You have done foolishly. You have not kept the command of The LORD your God, with which HE commanded you. For then the LORD would have established your kingdom over Israel forever.' But now, because of your impatience, your kingdom will not endure; The LORD has sought out a man after HIS own heart and appointed him leader of HIS people, <u>because you have not kept The</u> <u>LORD'S command</u>.'"** Saul gave into the feeling of impatience and it caused him to be disobedient. This cost Saul the Kingship and the Kingdom. What a high cost Saul paid, due to a feeling

The said fact is that Saul had almost made it. He was at the seventh day-the time that Prophet Samuel had set by The LORD'S command-if only Saul would have held out just a little bit longer, his blessing would not have been transferred to another.

Saul's impatience led to his disobedience and because he <u>did not honor</u> GOD"S commands in HIS heart, Saul lost the kingship, the blessing that JEHOVAH God had hand-selected him for. How tragic this day must have been, not only for Saul, but also for Saul's family and his descendants too. Saul was no longer considered royalty in God's eyes, but now he was rejected. He lost the throne not only for himself, but he had also just changed the destinies of his sons and their future generations forever. See how one impulsive, bad decision can affect your entire life? See what high costs are attached to disobedience? You may say well, I will repent and ask GOD to forgive me. HE will forgive, but it is HIS decision to restore or remove; and in this case, he removed Saul. It is far better to obey.

Proverbs 14:12 states,
**"There is a way *that seems* right to a man,
But its end *is* the way of death."**

This Scripture is so very vital, it shows us that our ways, our thoughts seem right, but by following our own thoughts, our destination is death.

In St. John 14:15 it states, "If you love ME, you will obey what I command." Which then means the opposite is true, if you disobey...then you must consider if you really love HIM. We can't pick and choose which commands that we will obey.

*Chosen Ones read The Bible and apply Its teachings to their lives. Obedience is a master key in our walk with our LORD.

And again in St. John 14:21 it states," Whoever has MY commands and obeys them, he is the one who loves ME."

1 Peter 2:9-10, lets us know that God considers us royalty just as Saul once was. It states," **But you are a <u>chosen generation</u>, a royal priesthood, a holy nation, HIS own special people, that you may proclaim the praises of HIM who called you out of darkness into HIS marvelous light; who once**

were not a people but are now the people of God, who had not obtained mercy but now have obtained mercy." As GOD'S royal and Chosen, we must be what the Bishop of Christian International, Bishop Bill Hamon, the Bishop and founder of the organization that I belong to, Christian International, says in a catchy phrase: we must be" rigidly righteous."

Let us learn from Saul's example; we cannot let the feeling of impatience rule in our lives. Impatience caused Saul to be disobedient and to rebel against the Word of GOD as the highest authority in his life and caused him instead to choose to do things his own way, which cost him dearly.

Eventually Saul found out that Samuel had gone to Jesse's house, David's dad, and anointed David in his place. Saul had to live out the rest of his days knowing the sad fact that he was now rejected by God from what was once his own blessing and there was nothing, nothing he could do about it. If Saul would have just waited-waited a little longer, just a few more hours, what a difference it would have made, what a totally different ending he would have had to his life and also that of his sons. His kingdom would have endured for all time- the honor of having The Messiah born in his lineage would have been his-but now, it was taken from him and given to another because of a feeling. David and his descendants were given the kingship and the honor of having The Messiah born in their lineage, receiving an everlasting Kingdom.

*Don't let impatience push you into doing something you will surely regret. That is the enemy's whole objective, to get you to act outside of GOD'S timing and to cause you to forfeit your blessing! It is a trick, a trap, a scheme from the kingdom of darkness. If you allow the spirit of impatience to dictate to you, and push you, remember, just like Saul, The LORD has a David willing and ready to receive your blessing. It is better to be still and wait on GOD. Obedience is the strategy that Mary taught us and as JESUS' mom, she most likely knew JESUS better than anyone else on earth. *Chosen Ones are like Mary; **we do what HE tells us.**

Secret #5 Be Vigilant in Prayer!

THE Chosen ONE, JESUS, The Christ

Colossians 4:2 "Continue earnestly in prayer, being vigilant in it with thanksgiving;

Matthew 26:41 "Watch and pray, lest you enter into temptation. The spirit is indeed willing, but the flesh is weak."

The definition of the word vigilant from the Merriam Webster Dictionary means alertly watchful especially to avoid danger. It suggests an intense-like watchfulness. Watch, or be alert, is mentioned over twenty times in the New Testament.

*As a Chosen One prayer is not an option, it is a necessity for daily spiritual survival.

During the time of CHRIST'S physical life on earth, the Roman Empire occupied and controlled the Israeli territory. They segmented the day & night into an equal number of hours and called them watches; there are four Roman watches. As mentioned earlier, Chosen One's are usually awakened very early in the morning for prayer, fitting the pattern of JESUS CHRIST'S prayer life. The fourth Roman watch was from 3AM-6AM; this is the prayer watch of the Chosen.

Mark 1:35, "Now in the morning, having risen <u>a long</u> <u>while before daylight</u>, HE went out and departed to a solitary place; and there HE prayed."
And
King David in Psalm 5:3, "My voice YOU shall hear in the morning, O LORD, In the morning I will direct it to YOU and I will look up."
And
Psalm 119:147, "I rise before the dawning of the morning And cry for help; I hope in YOUR Word."

Job 38:12 has had a significant impact on my prayer life. It states, **"Have you commanded the morning since your days began, and caused the dawn to know its place, that it might take hold of the ends of the earth, and the wicked be shaken out of it?"**

With our early morning prayers, we take dominion, authority over the current day. All the wicked plans, schemes and tactics that have been released against us for that day and prayerfully any in our future, are cancelled as we establish, with our prayers, The LORD'S dominion and authority in the earth and over our lives:

"Thy Kingdom come, Thy will be done on Earth, as it is in Heaven."

It is during this fourth watch, that our prayers are powerful in tearing down the astral altars and any other ungodly connections and wicked schemes that the adversary's agents have programmed into the heavenlies against us with their chanting and curses. We use this time to decree and establish peace for our lives and good outcomes for ourselves and our families; **"to call those things which be not are not as though they were" (Romans 4:17),** and watch them be established in our lives.

*Chosen Ones push past the temptation to stay in bed; we know that we have to be on duty daily at our prayer time established by Heaven. When Chosen Ones pray, Heaven hears and responds. A Chosen Ones prayer life is critical to overcoming every challenging circumstance, not only for us and for our families, but also for the Body of CHRIST.

Apostle Paul exhorts us to always pray in **Ephesians 6:18, "praying always with all prayer and supplication** (the action of asking earnestly), **in the Spirit, being watchful to this end with all perseverance and supplication for all the saints."**

JESUS told us the parable of the **"Unjust Judge" in Luke 18:1-8.** In it, HE established a very important principle for us.

"Then He spoke a parable to them, that men always ought to pray and not lose heart, saying: "There was in a certain city a judge who did not fear God nor regard man. Now there was a widow in that city; and she came to him, saying, 'Get justice for

me from my adversary.' And he would not for a while; but afterward he said within himself, 'Though I do not fear God nor regard man, yet because this widow troubles me I will avenge her, lest by her continual coming she weary me.' " Then the Lord said, 'Hear what the unjust judge said. And shall God not avenge His own elect who cry out day and night to Him, though He bears long with them? I tell you that He will avenge them speedily. Nevertheless, when the Son of Man comes, will He really find faith on the earth?"

From this parable we can plainly see that if we keep knocking, keep coming in prayer with our requests and not give up, we will surely receive our answers.

*Chosen Ones do not give up; we believe and continue to pray and decree the Word of the LORD until our answers show up.

Using the Scriptures in your prayers will definitely get GOD's attention. In Isaiah **55:10-11**, it is written:

"For as the rain comes down, and the snow from heaven, and do not return there, but water the earth, and make it bring forth and bud, that it may give seed to the sower, and bread to the eater, so shall My word be that goes forth from My mouth;
It shall not return to Me void, But it shall accomplish what I please, And it shall prosper *in the thing* for which I sent it."

When I graduated from my dietetic internship, because I lacked experience as a dietitian, it was very challenging to find a position. An ex-fellow intern told me about where she worked and that the company was hiring. The position was in a different county, but I couldn't let that be a deterrent, so I drove the distance, put in the application and returned later for the appointed interview. When I didn't hear back directly, I started to get anxious. I had three children, and we were barely getting by on my temporary positions that I was working through a temporary agency.

One evening, I was cooking dinner and I thought of the parable of the Unjust Judge. I said to myself, "I am going to do the same thing. I really need this job, so I am going to pray every 15 minutes until The LORD says something to me." Just like clockwork, I would cook for a few minutes, put the stirring spoon down, go into my bedroom and get on my knees and start asking GOD for the job. On the third visit to the bedroom, after kneeling, I said "LORD," before I could get any further, I heard HIM plainly say, "Get up off of your knees and quit begging, the job is yours." I said, "oh, okay, thank YOU!" A few days later, I received a phone call offering the position. I was so happy, so relieved. Praise the Living, Almighty GOD!

Now, after many years when I have thought about what GOD said, HE said to quit begging. I thought that it was kind of mean until the HOLY SPIRIT revealed to me that I was not a beggar but the child of THE KING. I could decree a thing in JESUS' name, and it would be mine. I wasn't supposed to treat GOD like the unjust judge, but instead like my Father who gives good and perfect gifts. HE knew I had need of a real position, a real job with a stable income, and HE had made a way for me. I give HIM all the praise for HIS faithfulness; HE has been absolutely faithful all these years and has taken very good care of us. I am so grateful.

Prayer absolutely works. I recently heard the acronym, P-U-S-H regarding prayer. It stands for P-Pray, U-Until, S-Something, H-Happens.

Ephesians 6:18, "Praying always with all prayer and supplication in the Spirit and watching thereunto with all perseverance and supplication for all saints."

Secret #6: By The Word of Our Testimony:

Chosen Ones Read, Meditate and Speak HIS Word!

John 1:1-9 states," In the beginning was the Word, and the Word was with God, and the Word was God. He was in the beginning with God. All things were made through Him, and without Him nothing was made that was made. In Him was life, and the life was the light of men. And the light shines in the darkness, and the darkness did not comprehend it."

Revelation 12:11 "And they overcame him by the Blood of The Lamb and By The Word of their Testimony, and they did not love their lives to the death."

John 1:14 "<u>And the Word became flesh</u> and dwelt among us, and we beheld His glory, the glory as of the only begotten of the Father, full of grace and truth."

John's Witness: The True Light

"There was a man sent from God, whose name *was* John. This man came for a witness, to bear witness of the Light, that all through him might believe. He was not that Light, but *was sent* to bear witness of that Light. That was the true Light which gives light to every man coming into the world." John 1:6-9.

Chosen Ones are true witnesses sent on assignment from God.

*The Chosen witness must know the ONE who sent him to be able to give others a true and accurate account. Every word matters.

When you give someone "your word" you are making a solemn pledge, a promise to do as you have spoken. GOD is the same, HE is held to HIS Word.

Psalm 138:2, "I will worship toward Your holy temple, And praise Your Name for Your lovingkindness and Your truth: for You have magnified Your Word above all Your name."

*Chosen Ones must practice being truthful; this will cause others to believe our testimonies of JESUS Christ.

"We overcome him by the Blood of the Lamb and by the word of our testimony."
(Revelations 12:11)

Testimony. When a person is called as a witness in the court, he is seated in the witness box, sworn in to tell the whole truth and then placed under a process of examination by the judge and jury. Everything about the witness is under scrutiny by all in the courtroom. It is the job of the witness to testify to the facts of what was specifically witnessed: what he saw, what he knows and what he experienced. In order for the witness to be deemed as credible, the experience and the words of the witness must be received as authentic; for they will be weighed by everyone listening and will determine the credibility, the reliability, the truthfulness of the witness. The lawyer tries only to place credible and reliable witnesses in the witness box to strengthen his case.

The principle is same with us: *JESUS needs HIS Chosen Ones to be reliable, credible and trustworthy witnesses to state HIS case in the earth and strengthen HIS cause and further the establishment of HIS Kingdom.

Isaiah 43:10 states, "You are my witnesses, says the LORD, and MY servant whom I have chosen, that you may know and believe ME and understand that I AM HE. Before ME there was no God formed, nor shall there be after ME."

True witnesses for The LORD have experienced HIS Word coming to pass in their lives. True witnesses can honestly speak of HIS goodness and mercies and can authentically share with others what great things HE has done from their own personal treasure boxes of blessings and miracles in their lives, starting with the gift of salvation.

As Chosen Ones, our testimonies remain sure and true as we persevere and endure, staying steadfast and unmovable on CHRIST, the Solid Rock, the Foundation of our lives. Our testimonies increase in number over time and strengthen as our faith continues to grow as we overcome bigger and larger tests and trials as the purposes for our lives unfold.

Because we each have and have had our own experiences with our FATHER, we are true witnesses and are able to give a real and accurate account that will lead others to the Cross of CHRIST and testimonies that will strengthen and encourage others.

JESUS' Words are containers that hold valuable information as well as almighty power!

*As Chosen Witnesses, we invoke HIS power as we decree HIS Words in the earth. **Proverbs 18:21 tells us "Death and life are in the power of the tongue…"**

*Chosen Ones read and meditate on God's Words which the HOLY SPIRIT brings back to our remembrance at the right time. We use prayer, another use of the word testify, as in speaking, which is our personal prayer words along with the written WORD of GOD to wage war against the enemy and his cohorts. In prayer, GOD strengthens us as we pour out ourselves before HIM. GOD'S words give us the delegated mighty power and authority to stand and to speak peace into challenging situations, and additionally to change the outcomes of situations by speaking what HE says instead of what the situation presents as.

We overcome by the Word of our Testimony. Our testimony, what we are speaking, what we are testifying to, will eventually manifest in our lives as we continue to decree and establish it in the earth through HIS HOLY WORD.

We know that Scripture, GOD'S Word trumps all. In it, another characteristic of HIS WORD, is revealed. A Scripture mentioned earlier, **Isaiah 55:10-11** -HIS WORDS travel. HIS WORDS travel to our past, to forgive us and heal us of past transgressions and past hurts. HIS WORDS travel to our futures and begins to establish or build what HE has decreed and declared over our lives. As we agree with HIM and decree and declare HIS WORD over challenging circumstances, from our position of authority in HIM, we watch as each situation bends, bows and submits itself to GOD'S Almighty power that is released through HIS spoken WORD. What a great honor to be able to speak HIS WORD with authority.

Another example of HIS Traveling WORD is found in **Matthew 8:5-9,13**. This is the account of JESUS healing a centurion's servant. It states, **"Now when Jesus had entered Capernaum, a centurion came to Him, pleading with Him, saying 'Lord, my servant is lying at home, dreadfully tormented.' And Jesus said to him, 'I will come and heal him.' The centurion answered and said, 'Lord, I am not worthy that You should come under my roof. But only speak** a word, and my servant will be healed. For I also am a man under authority, having soldiers under me. And I say to this one, 'go' and he goes, and to another, 'come' and he comes; and to my servant, 'Do this,' and he does it. Then Jesus said to the centurion, 'Go your way; and as you have believed, so let it be done for you.' And his servant was healed that same hour." HIS traveling WORD!

One last Scripture that we will look at for this section is **Joshua 1:8.** In this Scripture GOD lays out the tablet of how we can have sure success. It states, "**This Book of The Law shall not depart from your mouth, but you shall meditate in it day and night, that you may observe to do according to all that is written in it. For then you will make your way prosperous, and then you will have good success.**"

So in the Bible, we have The Law of Success. IF we keep the commands of the LORD and follow The Law of Success, it will absolutely work for us. So, let us look at this Scripture a little closer.

The LORD says 1) it shall not depart from your mouth-so we have to speak what The WORD says; 2) mediate in it-we have to read it, think about it and ponder on it-as we do this it gets in our hearts and becomes what we live by-becoming that sure rock-solid foundation, next, 3) it says- do according to all that is written in it- so we do what it says! So, we think about it, we speak it, and then we do it, we apply what it says to our lives and then we are promised that our ways will be prosperous and not only successful **BUT** it says good success. Here, in HIS WORD we have sure counsel, sure advice for how we can have successful lives, along with peace, joy and security-the instructions? it's all in The WORD of GOD.

Secret #7: Wage War with your Personal Prophecies.

Based on Chosen Ones: Apostle Paul and his spiritual son, Timothy.

Ezekiel 37:4-7 "Again He said to me, 'Prophesy to these bones, and say to them, O dry bones, hear the word of the LORD! Thus says the Lord GOD to these bones: Surely I will cause breath to enter into you, and you shall live. I will put sinews on you and bring flesh upon you, cover you with skin and put breath in you; and you shall live. Then you shall know that I *am* the LORD.'"

"So I prophesied as I was commanded; and as I prophesied, there was a noise, and suddenly a rattling; and the bones came together, bone to bone. Indeed, as I looked, the sinews and the flesh came upon them, and the skin covered them over; but *there was* no breath in them."

Ezekiel 37:10," So I prophesied as He commanded me, and breath came into them, and they lived, and stood upon their feet, an exceedingly great army."

Since we have the same creative power of the HOLY SPIRIT at work within us, we too can prophesy and create life to seemingly dead situations. The LORD GOD instructed Ezekiel to prophesy to dead bones; the bones went through a process and then eventually they took on flesh and eventually breath.

As we decree the WORD of the LORD over our situations with faith, the WORD becomes flesh and dwells among us, **John 1:14**. According to **Hebrews 11:1**, to paraphrase, faith mixed with our words becomes a substance, something tangible, something physical that we can touch; the thing that we are hoping for taking on flesh- coming alive!

I Timothy 1:18 states," **This charge I commit to you, son Timothy, according to the prophecies previously made concerning you, that by them you may wage the good warfare"**

As we read in the previous strategy about the Word of our Testimony, Paul also gave instructions that we can glean from today about prophetic utterances.

Why did Apostle Paul use the word "warfare" in the above Scripture, I **Timothy 1:18**?

In **Ephesians 6:11-17,** Apostle Paul reveals to us who our fight, is against.

"Put on the whole armor of God, that you may be able to stand against the <u>wiles</u> of the devil. ¹² For we do not <u>wrestle</u> against flesh and blood, but against principalities, against powers, against the rulers of the darkness of this age, against spiritual *hosts* of wickedness in the heavenly *places*."

"Therefore take up the whole armor of God, that you may be able to withstand in the <u>evil day</u>, and having done all, to stand. Stand therefore, having girded your waist with truth, having put on the breastplate of righteousness, and having shod your feet with the preparation of the gospel of peace; above all, taking the shield of faith with which you will be able to quench all the fiery darts of the wicked one. And take the helmet of salvation, and the sword of the Spirit, which is the word of God;"

I define the evil day as the time when you are under severe spiritual attack. These evil attacks, have one goal…to drive you away from GOD.

In **1 Corinthians Chapter 12**, the gift of prophecy is listed. GOD has given this gift to edify, (build us up), to comfort us, (in our time of need), and to exhort us, (to urge us onward in CHRIST), as **I Corinthians 14:3** states.

Paul instructed Timothy to wage a good warfare with his own personal prophecies; as Chosen Ones, we must do the same.

In **II Corinthians 13:1,** as a safeguard for each of us concerning receiving and applying personal prophecies to our lives, be wise and use this rule that The Bible states, **"This will be the third time I am coming to you. <u>By the mouth of two</u> <u>or three witnesses every word shall be established</u>."**

When the Holy Spirit has established a course of action for your life, The LORD will establish HIS plan for you through the mouth of two or three witnesses. After receiving a personal prophecy, you pray about it, meditate upon it and The LORD, through HIS Holy Spirit will reveal to you the way for the personal prophecy to be established in your life. HE may give you instructions, HE may give you directions. Since man is not perfect, it is always best to seek the Face of the LORD in prayer. I always ask HIM to speak to me in a way that I can understand because I do not want to miss HIS best for my life. I absolutely want the three witnesses instead of even two, before moving forward, especially in large undertakings; I have to know that HE is with me. This reminds me of what Moses said to GOD in **Exodus 33:15**: **"Then he said to Him, If Your Presence does not go with us, do not bring us up from here."** I feel the same way, if God is not going, I am not going either!

Now it is time for you "to wage warfare" with your personal prophetic word just like Apostle Paul taught his spiritual son Timothy. As we stand and war with our prophecies, The WORD of The LORD will surely prevail. I read my prophecies over and over, putting them before The LORD, as the HOLY SPIRIT leads me; I have read some so often I have them in my mind all the time and I am actively watching, looking for "the evidence of the thing not seen." Any movement I see in my life causing the prophetic word to come to pass, I work with it; that is, I work with it by pressing into prayer concerning it and launching out and taking action as directed. As we press and continue to pray, fast, read our Bible and declare the WORD of the LORD, we will see it materialize from the spiritual realm, take on flesh in our lives as the Scripture in Ezekiel speaks of.

*No matter how much time has passed, Chosen Ones continue to decree the WORD of the LORD and the personal prophecies that have been spoken over our lives. Even if the situation appears dead, "these bones can live." The LORD GOD can and will breathe on the situation and give it life at the appointed time. So, we press in, we fight on, and we continue to declare the Word of Truth.

Romans 16:20 states, **"And the God of Peace will crush satan under your feet shortly. The grace of our Lord Jesus Christ be with you. Amen."**

One Wednesday evening, right before our corporate prayer, I was under a strong spiritual attack in my mind, and I felt a strong wave against my body pushing against me – a strong feeling of being worn out. I pressed on and oversaw the prayer that evening, only to find out that everyone who attended was sensing and going through the same thing. Praises be to GOD, after our hour of corporate prayer, we were back on sure footing; we were energized and revitalized through prayer. I realized that we were getting very close to our very large breakthroughs and the enemy sent an onslaught against us to try and deter us, to make us give up! We must stay the course!

*Chosen Ones must press on, stay stable and stay faithful.

From this example, we can plainly see that the enemy knew that we were very close to obtaining the answers to our prayers, so he launched a counterattack against us.

As long as we are armed with the aforementioned battle gear, stated by Apostle Paul in **Ephesians chapter 6,** we will stand and be able to quench all the fiery darts of the enemy; everything he tries will fail against us. Praise the Holy Name of JESUS!

The LORD has promised us that HE will crush satan under our feet, so that is satan's position, even in the evil day, no matter how we feel, as long as we stand.

We have to remember that it is a day by day, decision by decision journey, and walk of faith.

*As we are confronted with temptations and challenges, Chosen Ones choose what would make JESUS proud even if it costs us personally. It is a process, but as the Scripture above says The LORD will crush him "shortly."

This is where **James 1:2-4** is vital to our spiritual growth. **"My brethren, count it all joy when you fall into various trials, knowing that the testing of your faith produces patience. But let patience have its perfect work, that you may be perfect and complete, lacking nothing."**

*This is why Chosen Ones do not get offended at GOD when challenges come.

Chosen Ones know that The LORD is producing patience which brings about endurance in our spirits, which in turn will allow us to finish our race. **Matthew 24:13 states, "But he who endures to the end shall be saved."** Chosen Ones have their eyes on the finish line.

We will be ones who echo the words of Apostle Paul in **II Timothy 4:7-8," I have fought the good fight, I have finished the race, I have kept the faith. Finally, there is laid up for me the crown of righteousness, which the Lord, the righteous Judge, will give to me on that Day, and not to me only but also to all who have loved His appearing."**

Conclusion

GOD is faithful! **"HE will strengthen and protect you from the evil one"****, (II Thessalonians 3:3),** as you continue to fight the good fight daily.

HE is the definition of faithfulness; that is a big part of HIS character forever, faithful. Because of **Malachi 3:6,** we know that HE does not change! Because of this truth, we can always count on HIM to fulfill HIS Word personally in each of our lives.

Receiving truths about the ways that the Chosen Ones who have gone on before us faced challenges but overcame, as you have read, is absolutely priceless! The LORD made sure that their life events and the wisdom they applied were written down and preserved for us. The best thing that we can do for ourselves is to apply these revealed truths to our lives so that we will then be successful.

*Chosen Ones keep coming to JESUS' Throne Daily!

This is one of the most important strategies in gaining the advantage daily. If you keep showing up to the battle, you are already at least at the half-way point to the victory.

I exhort you: This day, make HOLY SPIRIT led decisions; this day forgive everyone who has caused offense in your heart; this day live a righteous lifestyle. Then tomorrow, start again because tomorrow is now "this day."

Additionally, do not let what has transpired in the past hold you back in chains; yesterday is gone, over! Yesterday is now a memory! Take what you have learned from your yesterdays" and <u>MOVE</u> forward!

In conclusion, once again looking at the Scripture in Joshua, The LORD gave Joshua the greatest secret to success. After Moses died, The LORD commissioned Joshua, a

Chosen One, to take his place. As Joshua looked out over the mass of people that he was now responsible for before GOD, The LORD spoke to him and gave Joshua these instructions:

Joshua 1:7-8, "Only be strong and very courageous, that you may observe to do according to all the law which Moses My servant commanded you; do not turn from it to the right hand or to the left, that you may prosper wherever you go. This Book of the Law shall not depart from your mouth, but you shall meditate in it day and night, that you may observe to do according to all that is written in it. For then you will make your way prosperous, and then you will have good success."

May The LORD GOD HIMSELF bless you and keep you- HIS Chosen ONE.

Made in the USA
Columbia, SC
19 May 2025

58045819R00062